Reclaiming Enduring Success:
Living Beyond Fear

(365 Daily Empowering Success Quotes & Personal Growth Exercises)

Aiming to Heal

Copyright 2024
Chistell Publishing
https://www.chistell.com
First Printing, May 2024

All rights reserved

Published by: Chistell Publishing
                 7235 Aventine Way, Suite #201
                 Chattanooga, TN 37421

Author: Denise Turney
ISBN: 979-8-9856651-6-1

Dedication

Aiming to Heal

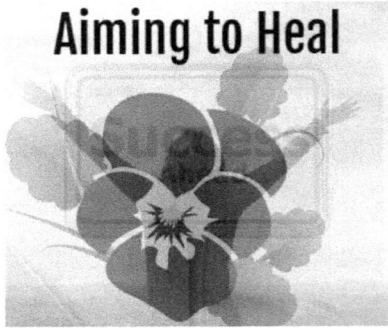

For my son

I love you, Gregory –

Table of Contents

"Love is the greatest light. It's impossible to be lost while in the light of love."

Achieving Enduring Success: Living Beyond Fear

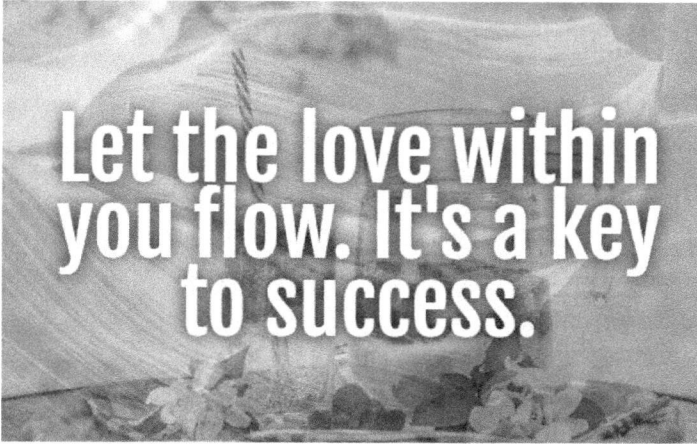

Let the love within you flow. It's a key to success.

Achieving success is easy once you move beyond fear. Yet, in this context the word "easy" seems like a trick. Why? Getting free of fear once and for all, so that it never returns, can be a bit of work.

The mind can project fear into many different forms. For example, you could feel afraid of an animal, perhaps your neighbor's dog or cat. Or you could project fear onto a person, an event, money, a room, the sound of someone's voice, a location or even a thought.

Forms that your mind could use to project fear may be near endless. You'll know when this is happening. During these instances you'll feel as if you're going from one challenge to another, from one upset to another.

Should this continue for years, as it often does, you could start to feel exhausted, maybe hopeless. It wouldn't be a shock if life started to feel unfair to you, as if life itself was bullying you and all because fear had you in a grip.

If you don't make the link between stress, worry, and unhappiness to fear, you could spin your wheels trying to fix one projected fear form after another. Once you "fix" one form, your mind projects fear into a different form, pushing peace, joy, and enduring success away from you, keeping you lost, wondering what's happening.

Achieving Enduring Success: Living Beyond Fear aims to help you take a closer look at what's happening in your life, helping you to identify fear's success roadblocks. Another advantage the book aims to help you gain is to become increasingly familiar with fear, what it feels like, when it's beginning to surface in your mind, and how you could stop fear in its tracks early.

As with any inner work, to make gains you'll have to practice honesty with yourself. Along the way, you might feel stuck or stretched. Should this occur, consider working with a licensed, experienced, and ethical therapist.

Additionally, take your time working through **Achieving Enduring Success: Living Beyond Fear.** Focus on each of the 365 quotes in the book. These are short writings that are intended to have an impact. It's like how a short exclamation or proclamation can capture your attention for hours, fueling you with emotion and thought. Words are, indeed, powerful.

Accompanying the short writings, you will find an introspection section. Here is where you shouldn't rush. Honesty and time can prove to be good friends at this point in **Achieving Enduring Success: Living Beyond Fear**.

Hopefully, before you're halfway through the book, you'll start to notice that, just as your mind projects fear in countless forms and situations, it's also your mind that is key to your healing, to you moving beyond fear into love and enduring success.

Enjoy **Achieving Enduring Success: Living Beyond Fear**, the short writings, and the rewarding work ahead. Most of all, enjoy gaining freedom from fear and living a life of continual success, joy, and peace – what you are intended to experience and treasure!

"On a clear day eternity is seen above the horizon."

Chapter 1 – Clarity is Power

Clarity is a powerful success tool, keeping your goal present while lighting the path from where you are now to where you're headed. Clarity. Imagine that. A success tool.

This goes against the belief that excessive exertion, also known as "hard work", is the pathway to success. Much of this thinking may be driven by commerce, the belief that money is a "savior", and the false concept that you only have value when someone else tells you that you do – indeed -- have *real* value.

Should you see money as a "savior" and, even more, should you place increasing value on money based on how much you have, you could, in turn, give more value to people who have a lot of money. It took me years to realize how easy it is to get lost in this thinking, drifting further away from what you entered this world to do. It started when I was young.

"Get a job!" my father told me after I hit the magical age of 15 years. A year later, I was working a full-time job, running track, and attending school full-time. The gig was at a coffee shop, a place where I filled in as cashier, hostess, and food server.

The job wasn't hard; it didn't pay much either. More than anything, I learned how bringing in your own money can make other people feel happiness. All at once, it was as if, simply by working a paying job, I was doing something good – as if I had suddenly become, somehow -- better.

Seeing how getting a job affected my father and my elders, making them proud, I started to create beliefs around money that have, at times, held me back. Much of my belief around work and money is embedded in ancestral proclamations. "Work hard and you'll always have a job." Or "Work hard and you'll always be able to find a job."

Before I knew it, my days were filled with work. After I moved out of my father's house, it was "Hello, bills!" time. With this came the assurance that I had no choice but to work to get enough money to pay my bills, which took me further away from what I truly knew I had come into this world to do (write books).

Want real success in this world? Don't do what I did. Although I'm getting on track, a lot of years passed with me grinding it out on jobs I knew weren't on my success path.

For me, drifting away from my path, what I knew with clarity that I was here to do, happened slowly. A lot of it was born in my elders' and my acceptance of the 40-hour workweek.

Believe it or not, in the United States, the National Labor Union was one of the earliest organizations to push for an eight-hour workday, not because they wanted people to work more. They pushed for an eight-hour workday because many Americans were working long hours; those in manufacturing worked 100 hours or more each week.[1]

Good-bye work-life balance. And good-bye success path. Now, you're working just to keep a job so you can pay bills. Do this long enough and the clarity you once had about your success path may evaporate.

On the other hand, there could be another reason why you drifted away from your success path, losing clarity about what you *truly* want. You might have simply gotten distracted. In this world of distractions, lack of clarity can happen within months.

As an example, you might admire someone so much that you shelve your success dreams so that you can pursue what the person you admire wants you to do instead. This happens with parents and children, spouses, managers and employees, ministers and protegees, and community workers.

You don't have to fall into this trap. In fact, you can live free of this by practicing awareness, respecting your success path, stirring up courage, and being honest. Regarding honesty, admit what you're feeling. Take a close look at why you're doing what you do.

Disallow illusions to get buried in your subconscious, hiding, and muddying your inner vision – robbing you of clarity. Be honest with yourself. Avoid trying to convince yourself that you should experience happiness doing what you don't want to do but think you should do just to avoid something (e.g., questions from someone you admire, teasing).

Just like you don't have to like eating marshmallows simply because other people do, you don't have to like doing what your elders or peers tell you to do. More importantly, you don't have to lie to yourself and tell yourself you like something you don't.

Honesty and clarity are twins; they roll together. To enter success, get clear about what you want. Be honest about what you're feeling. Gain clarity around "why" you're doing what you're currently doing and "why" you want to do what you clearly know is right for you (if it's not what you're doing now).

Here's how you could gain clarity about what you truly want, what you know at your core is right for you:

- Write about your goals, beliefs, including erroneous beliefs (also known as errors in thinking), and success attempts in a journal
- Revisit the "first" times you felt a surge of joy. What were you doing?
- Enjoy a nature walk in a safe area. See if inner vision surfaces while out walking or during a night dream after you return from your walk.
- Type a list of activities that interest you. Pay attention to what you feel as you create the list. See if one or more of the activities light a spark within you.

On the next pages are motivating quotes to help keep you on track as it regards getting clear about what you truly want to experience. Let these short writings power you up for the success that's ahead for you. Focus on a different quote each day.

Resources:

1. A History of How the 40-Hour Workweek Became the Norm in America (businessinsider.com)

Get Clear About What You _Really_ Want

Not only do you need a clear path to success, but you already have one. It's inside of you.

Darts thrown in the dark rarely hit their target.

Clarity demands honesty.

Only the author knows what she meant to write.

Have you felt it? Seen it? There's a light in you.

Joy is a brilliant guide.

Who wouldn't lostness fatigue? Get in the clearing.

Week in Review (Take your time filling this out. At the end of a year, you can notice good change.)

Which of this week's quotes resonated with you most?

_____

_____

_____

_____

Why did this quote resonate?

_____

_____

_____

_____

_____

List 3 promises you will make to yourself (and keep) to get clear about what you "really" want.

_____

_____

_____

_____

_____

_____

_____

_____

_____

_____

Break It Down

Success is like putting a thousand puzzle pieces together, allowing each piece to be magnificent.

A matter taken apart is less intimidating.

The most important step is the step you're taking now.

Look too far back, too far ahead and the view could become cloudy.

Inside the system is what keeps the whole running.

After this focus on the next step.

Distrust demands answers about the future.

Week in Review (Take your time filling this out. At the end of a year, you can notice good change.)

Which of this week's quotes resonated with you most?

_____

_____

_____

_____

Why did this quote resonate?

_____

_____

_____

_____

_____

List 3 promises you will make to yourself (and keep) to break apart what you need to do to get from where you are now to where you want to be. *Don't break your promises to yourself.*

_____

_____

_____

_____

_____

_____

_____

_____

_____

Look Again

Enter stillness and look again.

Each new glance reveals something original.

What you didn't see before matters.

Try again. Is the view clear?

The path is to discover your true Self.

Don't quit. You're worth another look.

With clarity comes a sure course.

Week in Review (Take your time filling this out. At the end of a year, you can notice good change.)

Which of this week's quotes resonated with you most?

_____

_____

_____

_____

Why did this quote resonate?

_____

_____

_____

_____

_____

What 4 specific actions can you take to start to look at life, including a goal you're passionate about achieving, differently, inviting in more clarity?

_____

_____

_____

_____

_____

_____

_____

_____

_____

_____

Let It Open

It's remarkable how the path opens after you take the first core step.

Let the way open before you.

Of its own accord light pours through.

Trust and watch what happens.

Courage is an open window.

Rest awhile. The door will open.

Attain - many have. You can too.

Week in Review (Take your time filling this out. At the end of a year, you can notice good change.)

Which of this week's quotes resonated with you most?

_____

_____

_____

_____

Why did this quote resonate?

_____

_____

_____

_____

_____

List two routines and habits you know are holding you back. How are you going to end these habits and start new, healthy, success-focused habits?

_____

_____

_____

_____

_____

_____

_____

_____

_____

_____

What's There?

Meditate. Pray. Clear your chakras. Reach your core.
What's there?

Don't be afraid to look within.

Reflections are not mirrors to the soul.

Prove to yourself what's within.

A shadow in passing is not what you are.

What if success brings you closer to the truth?

Keep going. You're getting to know yourself.

Week in Review (Take your time filling this out. At the end of a year, you can notice good change.)

Which of this week's quotes resonated with you most?

_____

_____

_____

_____

Why did this quote resonate?

_____

_____

_____

_____

_____

There's meditation, prayer, nature walks and more. List two specific actions you are going to take each day to tap into your inner or Higher Self.

_____

_____

_____

_____

_____

_____

_____

_____

_____

_____

"Discovering the 'why' is a first step toward success."

Chapter 2 – Identify the Why

It's impossible to have total clarity about what you are trying to do without an understanding of "why" you want to achieve a goal. Your "why" may be your greatest motivation, particularly during times when you feel pressed, challenged, and willing to quit.

Discovering the why behind what you want to do necessitates that you pose questions to yourself. To begin, ask yourself when was the first time that the desire surfaced? How old were you when you first wanted to achieve the goal? And how did the desire formulate or introduce itself to your consciousness?

For example, did the desire initially formulate as a dream? Did it surface during a conversation, while you were watching a movie, reading a book, or listening to a song? If so, do you hold strong emotions or thoughts regarding the singer or songwriter, actress, writer, people who appeared in the dream?

How could your feeling about those people influence your perceptions about the goal? This is important because, considering that life experiences connect, you could be hiding important truths within a desire.

Years ago, I felt this intense attraction to enter a relationship. The attraction was overwhelming, so strong that I knew an unhealed part of me was pushing me toward the relationship. Turns out that the man I felt the intense attraction for drank alcohol to the point of intoxication. My family had a history of that, and I didn't hide that from myself. Taking the time to examine the attraction and discover the "why" for the desire to pursue the relationship prevented me from making a colossal mistake. If I hadn't looked deeper at the desire, I could be dwelling in a pool of regret.

So, invest the time to discover your "why". You'll be glad that you did.

Back to those questions. Here are several questions you can ask yourself to start probing, surfacing the why behind what you want to achieve.

What do you love to do to the point that simply engaging in this activity feels like ample reward, a rich payment?

Is there something that makes time feel as if it doesn't exist when you're doing it? What is that something?

How do you want to be remembered? In other words, what images, emotions, and thoughts do you want to automatically surface in others when they think of you?

Just what do you do well without investing much effort in the activity? What seems to come naturally to you?

Others may have complimented you on your passion or what you do well, perhaps even sharing with you how what you do blesses them. Avoid getting tangled in concern around how much income you could generate from your passion.

That's a good way to talk yourself out of what you want to do. Enough people already do that every single day. Don't join that habit, not if you want to succeed.

Another step you could take to reveal your "why" is to write about your life, as you imagine it would be, if your goal was already fulfilled. Get specific in your writings, detailing sights, sounds, scents, colors, and people you cross paths with as you live your "dream fulfilled" life.

Let yourself really feel the achievement. Then, go back and revisit the questions mentioned earlier in this chapter. Can you honestly say that none of your answers have changed? If they have, write those new responses down alongside the initial responses.

Compare the two. Also, give yourself a week to explore, probe, and surface your "why". After you identify your true "why" write it in a journal, on a spreadsheet, sheet of paper, or whiteboard, somewhere that you'll easily return to.

Your "why" is like fuel in an automobile. It's going to help get you from where you are now to where you want to be.

As with the previous chapter, on the next pages are empowering quotes that relate to your "why". Allow these short writings and the exercises on the next few pages to help you begin to use your "why" to take the next, best step forward.

Cause of Desire

Discover from where desire comes and you can glimpse the whole experience.

At some point, regardless of what you do, you must answer - why.

All growth starts at the root.

Ensure the root of your success dream is good.

Ever seen a matter flourish separated from its root?

Remove the root, remove the fruit.

Don't just nurture the leaves and fruit of your dreams, always care for the root of your success.

Week in Review (Take your time filling this out. At the end of a year, you can notice good change.)

Which of this week's quotes resonated with you most?

_____

_____

_____

_____

Why did this quote resonate?

_____

_____

_____

_____

_____

What is the "root" cause of your goal or success-desire? Give yourself time to consider this as the "why" of what you do or want to do is a key to achieving what you want.

_____

_____

_____

_____

_____

_____

_____

_____

_____

_____

Do You Believe in The Why?

There's a why behind everything.

Worldly storms ensure if you don't believe in the why, your dreams get flooded with sorrow.

Don't let a lifetime get buried in ignorance when it comes to why you do what you do.

Living close to your why is bliss.

There is no greater motivation than your why.

Remind yourself "why" you're doing what you do.

Believe in your "why" and nothing can stop you.

Week in Review (Take your time filling this out. At the end of a year, you can notice good change.)

Which of this week's quotes resonated with you most?

_____

_____

_____

_____

Why did this quote resonate?

_____

_____

_____

_____

_____

_____

Do you trust the "why"? Expound on the reason for your trust. Get it on paper. Revisiting what you write now weeks later can offer great motivation.

_____

_____

_____

_____

_____

_____

_____

_____

_____

_____

When The Why Expands

Life is from here to there to here to there to there –
forever expanding.

No bigger "why" than the one you've been given.

Your "why" has a longer life than you now know.

Do the work. Fulfill your dream and watch it expand.

Fulfilling your "why" is helping you build a legacy.

Plant the seed. Who knows when it will grow but grow
it will!

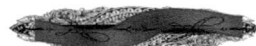

Do what deep within you promised.

Week in Review (Take your time filling this out. At the end of a year, you can notice good change.)

Which of this week's quotes resonated with you most?

_____

_____

_____

_____

Why did this quote resonate?

_____

_____

_____

_____

_____

What will you do if your "why" starts to expand and you start aiming to take on, achieve more?

_____

_____

_____

_____

_____

_____

_____

_____

_____

_____

Measuring Passion

Passion must be strong enough to weather the world's storms.

How deep is your passion?

This I believe – your dream will come true.

Soon you'll learn how deep and wide your passion is.

Passion is a fuel that energizes your greatest pursuit.

Help rests in the depths of your passion for your dream.

The passionate love what they do.

Week in Review (Take your time filling this out. At the end of a year, you can notice good change.)

Which of this week's quotes resonated with you most?

_____

_____

_____

_____

Why did this quote resonate?

_____

_____

_____

_____

At the start, passion is hot, but will it sustain itself or will it go out? Find out now before you invest energy and time into a dream that may end up only fading. Write about why you believe your passion for your dream is sufficient to get you through challenges, however many there end up being.

_____

_____

_____

_____

_____

_____

_____

_____

_____

Did Someone Send You?

The key is to remember that this is your life.

A life lived for someone else is not yours.

Do you know who you're striving for?

Each time you look over your shoulder, upon whom do you hope to gaze?

Run! Run! Run! But for who?

Other people's dreams aren't your master.

When it's over who will have been your life's architect?

Week in Review (Take your time filling this out. At the end of a year, you can notice good change.)

Which of this week's quotes resonated with you most?

_____

_____

_____

_____

Why did this quote resonate?

_____

_____

_____

_____

_____

Let a week pass before answering this question. Whose dream are you pursuing? Why can you honestly say that the dream isn't someone else's?

_____

_____

_____

_____

_____

_____

_____

_____

_____

_____

"Fear is an Illusion, less real than a dream."

Chapter 3 – Facing Fear

Between you and success is fear. If the divide between where you are now and the success that you long for feels too wide, don't worry. There's great news!

Fear is not real.

Howbeit, there's a challenge. You believe that fear is real. Because you give fear the illusion of power by investing in fear with belief and even, trust, you must *face fear* to cross the bridge from illusion to truth, to enjoy real success.

Your mind is so powerful that you can deceive yourself and believe that deception is real. Regarding fear, Marilyn Ferguson shared, "Ultimately we know deeply that the other side of every fear is freedom."

Samuel Butler had this to say about fear, "Fear is static that prevents me from hearing myself." Finally, there's Henry Ford who shared, "One of the greatest discoveries a man makes, one of his great surprises, is to find he can do what he was afraid he couldn't do."

Because fear isn't something you can touch, smell, or hear, you know it's a mental projection. It also might have become a habit.

Therefore, it's vital that you find out if you're in the habit of scaring yourself. Do you catastrophize ideas about the future? If so, are there emotions that you feel you're attracted to, hard emotions that feel good to you?

Those emotions are a payoff for investing in fear, for scaring yourself. In what other ways can you get this payoff? Start to explore new ways to feel excited, invigorated, or another emotion that fear might provide you with.

Another thing to consider is *when* you start to scare yourself. Do you imagine fearful images and experiences (perhaps you see yourself being embarrassed as you fail at what you're attempting to do) just before it's time to "start" doing what you want to do?

This may be at play if you struggle to get started with doing what you want to achieve. Or do you start to worry and continuously consider what could go wrong after you're in the middle of an achievement?

Should this be the case, perhaps you're certain that you can block or stop yourself if you do so at the middle of an experience. Then, it might be just before you manifest the success you've been striving for that you terrify yourself.

Look back over your life and see if you can spot *when* you start to scare yourself. Next, create small habits that shift you away from this habit. Examples of habits that could help you to shift in positive ways include journaling about past achievements and how you thought and felt as you started to fulfill your goals. Also, write about how you felt while you were in the middle of fulfilling a goal and how you felt when you had fully accomplished what you'd set out to achieve.

In addition to writing in a journal, you could take a different route to and from the store, to and from work, or to and from a friend's house. Changing your diet, drinking more water, going to bed earlier, dancing, and walking on a beach are other small habits you could introduce into your life to shift.

Singing aloud around friends, while you're riding an elevator, or walking down the sidewalk; riding a bicycle for the first time in years; entering an amateur sporting event; and helping to build a home or craft can also help you to shift.

The point is to introduce change into your life, good change. Start with small habits, allowing the habits to link. It's a good way to help your brain see that you are safe in a world of change and whether you realize it now or not, change is a huge part of success.

What Are You Afraid Of?

Fear may be present, but it must never lead.

There's a wall before you? Tell it to move. It's only fear.

How long are you going to hold yourself prisoner to fear?

The thing that's stopping you won't leave until you face it.

Fear will morph, shift, and change until you let it go.

How much longer before you release fear?

Here it comes again — the thing you keep running from.

Week in Review (Take your time filling this out. At the end of a year, you can notice good change.)

Which of this week's quotes resonated with you most?

_____

_____

_____

_____

Why did this quote resonate?

_____

_____

_____

_____

_____

What 3 things scare you about pursuing your dream? What 3 things scare you about what might happen after your dream comes true?

_____

_____

_____

_____

_____

_____

_____

_____

_____

_____

No Other Way

When you turn around and face what you've been fleeing it disappears.

Follow your success path and you'll move through fear.

Fear is a mountain high hurdle. Leap it.

Illusions are not real.

Fear cannot erase your destiny. You must fulfill it. There is no other way.

Take the courage route; it's the rewarding path.

What if the road to your success doesn't always feel safe? Will you still go?

Week in Review (Take your time filling this out. At the end of a year, you can notice good change.)

Which of this week's quotes resonated with you most?

_____

_____

_____

_____

Why did this quote resonate?

_____

_____

_____

_____

_____

Is your goal linked with your purpose? How so?

_____

_____

_____

_____

_____

_____

_____

_____

_____

_____

_____

Fear Is an Illusion

Fear's architect is only capable of designing illusions.

Stop engaging in magical thinking.

The thing you fear isn't real.

Fear is like a magic trick.

Illusions change shapes, changing form to form.

Run right through it – nothing that you fear is real.

What do you choose to believe, your Higher Self or fear?

Week in Review (Take your time filling this out. At the end of a year, you can notice good change.)

Which of this week's quotes resonated with you most?

_____

_____

_____

_____

Why did this quote resonate?

_____

_____

_____

_____

_____

Write about the one fear that you still believe in. Why do you believe this fear/illusion? How can you finally let the fear go?

_____

_____

_____

_____

_____

_____

_____

_____

_____

_____

Around and Around

Ruminating thoughts are circles. If you don't want to go around and around step out of them.

Fear will have you circling the mountain for nothing in return.

Stop chasing fearful thoughts.

You could convince yourself that you're out of the reach of success but why do that?

Thoughts mimic, breeding damaging doubt.

The fear merry-go-round is not a fun ride.

Straight ahead not around and around.

Week in Review (Take your time filling this out. At the end of a year, you can notice good change.)

Which of this week's quotes resonated with you most?

_____

_____

_____

_____

Why did this quote resonate?

_____

_____

_____

_____

_____

How long have you been ruminating? Study ruminating and how and why the brain repeats thoughts. Which two ruminations are you going to release?

_____

_____

_____

_____

_____

_____

_____

_____

_____

_____

Entering Stillness

Enter stillness. Rest here awhile.

Get still. Hear what you should do now?

Peace grows when you get still.

Folks say they hear the Creator speak in the stillness.

You don't have to "die" to get still, to live again.

Freedom from fear is stillness.

Answers are buried within stillness.

Week in Review (Take your time filling this out. At the end of a year, you can notice good change.)

Which of this week's quotes resonated with you most?

_____

_____

_____

_____

Why did this quote resonate?

_____

_____

_____

_____

_____

Commit to getting still twice a day. Write about your experiences after you've been getting still for 10 minutes twice a day for a week.

_____

_____

_____

_____

_____

_____

_____

_____

_____

_____

"Real success is living beyond fear."

Chapter 4 – Moving Beyond Fear

Although moving beyond fear may seem to occur step-by-step, you could move beyond fear in an instant. Moving beyond fear requires you to take full responsibility for your life. This means that you take full responsibility for what you think, say, do, perceive, and feel.

Admittedly, this isn't what the world says. The world tells you that what happens to you is someone else's doing. It's why you might feel frustrated, hopeless, or angry, perhaps even seeking someone to take these hard emotions out on, as if this other person were you, controlling what you say, do, think, perceive, and feel.

However, if you want to achieve your love-based goals, you must take full responsibility for your life. You must accept that *this is your life.*

Once you accept full responsibility for your life, examine when and how you scare yourself away from your "why", blocking yourself from achieving what you most want to do. Then, open a spreadsheet or get out your journal and write down one small action that you can take that will bring you closer to goal fulfillment.

For now, simply write the action down. Then, write down the next 10 steps that you can take to realize your dream. Again, don't concern yourself with what will happen after you complete each step.

Instead, simply record the steps. Next to each action, write down when you will take the action, including whether you will take the action in the morning, during noon or in the evening.

Also, write down resources, including people you need to contact, that are aligned with each action. Keep in mind that some actions simply need to be taken, no resources necessary – just your action.

Each love-based action that you take proves that you can trust yourself, proves that you do and will take care of yourself. So, get started. Your actions can help to free you from fear.

Signs Fear Is Holding You Hostage

Humanity's greatest prison warden is fear.

Erroneous repetition is a song called fear.

Have you seen this day before? How many times?

You can spend life *watching others* do what it takes to fulfill their destiny.

Confusion is everywhere when you're scared.

Jealousy is a weedlike crop rooted in fear.

Another person's opinion has become a god.

Week in Review (Take your time filling this out. At the end of a year, you can notice good change.)

Which of this week's quotes resonated with you most?

_____

_____

_____

_____

Why did this quote resonate?

_____

_____

_____

_____

_____

Think back. How did you feel the first time you felt afraid, as best as you can recall? How do you feel now when you experience fear? List two actions you can take to free yourself of these fear symptoms.

_____

_____

_____

_____

_____

_____

_____

_____

_____

Strategies to Overcome Fear

Honesty and courage open doors that take you away from fear.

Get as close as you can to your One True Self and fear will vanish.

Prayer is a friend to the truth seeker.

Doing what you think you can't challenges ego.

Let your inner light lead.

Recall challenges you've already overcome.

Desire for good is like a wind, thrusting you over the highest barrier.

Week in Review (Take your time filling this out. At the end of a year, you can notice good change.)

Which of this week's quotes resonated with you most?

_____

_____

_____

_____

Why did this quote resonate?

_____

_____

_____

_____

_____

Write about an instance when you overcame fear.

_____

_____

_____

_____

_____

_____

_____

_____

_____

_____

Small Actions Add Up

Small forward steps turn into miles.

Your really can only take one step at a time.

Focus on what you're doing right now.

Dwell too much on the future and confusion could set in.

Invest in what you're doing now, and a door will open.

You must finish this before you can start on that.

What if you must add enough good energy to the current stage of your life to advance?

Week in Review (Take your time filling this out. At the end of a year, you can notice good change.)

Which of this week's quotes resonated with you most?

_____

_____

_____

_____

Why did this quote resonate?

_____

_____

_____

_____

_____

What positive small actions that keep you in the "present" are you going to turn into habits, adding another resource to your success toolbox?

_____

_____

_____

_____

_____

_____

_____

_____

_____

What You Feel You Can Do

Look back. See all you've come through. Build confidence on this good history.

Go a little further than you think you can.

Let's get to the point. What do you think you can do?

Not all emotions reflect the truth.

Willingness to walk with discomfort can lead to great, new discoveries.

So far how many times have emotions betrayed you?

Who knows how much truth there is in what you're feeling.

Week in Review (Take your time filling this out. At the end of a year, you can notice good change.)

Which of this week's quotes resonated with you most?

_____

_____

_____

_____

Why did this quote resonate?

_____

_____

_____

_____

_____

Get honest with yourself. What do you believe you can achieve now, at this instant? What makes you believe you can do this? Explain how you could use this confidence to develop the belief that you can do something greater.

_____

_____

_____

_____

_____

_____

_____

_____

_____

Accept Truth and Be Free of Fear

Truth pulled me out of the madness of fear.

Truth and fear will forever remain on different sides of the road.

A little truth, a little fear won't work.

Fear won't season truth. It can't.

There is no middle ground, no blending of truth and fear.

Truth or fear, which you see is totally up to you.

You don't have to accept truth. However, you'll regret it if you don't.

Week in Review (Take your time filling this out. At the end of a year, you can notice good change.)

Which of this week's quotes resonated with you most?

_____

_____

_____

_____

Why did this quote resonate?

_____

_____

_____

_____

_____

Write about 3 things you once thought were true, but you now know aren't. Could you be wrong in believing that you can't achieve your great dream?

_____

_____

_____

_____

_____

_____

_____

_____

_____

_____

"Half-hearted success attempts offer no real reward."

Chapter 5 – Deliberate Success

Go after success "on purpose". Don't teeter; go straightway toward love-based success. If you're sincere about achieving success, you *can't also* make comfort your aim. You must truly desire the success that you say you want.

That means, if you need to telephone someone who has already succeeded at what you want to do, you push apprehension aside and make the telephone call. Or if you need to dine with a major influencer in your industry, you reach out to schedule the lunch until you land the meeting.

Time investment and effort expended is not your primary focus. Sure. You're smart and avoid slipping into workaholism. Another priority for you is ensuring that you get sufficient quality sleep at night.

But, if you had to choose between sleeping in so you can enjoy the warmth of being tucked beneath your comforter and getting up to design another anime episode (using anime as a passion example), you'd get out of bed, not once but over and over.

Comfort is not your aim. Success is.

You're smart about your time. Seeing the domino effect in a single decision that you make is easy for you to do. Furthermore, you're not expecting success to "magically" happen for you.

Instead of looking to "magic" you've identified specific resources you need to achieve success. You know how much financial backing you need, whether that money comes from your personal savings or is gained through a financial partnership.

Developing new products and services is common for you, powering your success as you are introduced to new readers, investors, shareholders, and/or shoppers. In fact, you might design your organization so that it will thrive for decades, perhaps centuries, after you have transitioned from this world.

Teeter-tottering, wobbling, and moving ahead half-heartedly is not for you. It's not what you do. Why? You're serious about achieving your goals. Not only do you have a clear inner vision as it regards living a successful life, but you also trust your Higher Self and you're following love-based inner vision.

Early Success

Getting started is the quickest way to achieve early success.

Waiting is a slow giving in to fear.

What's the first thing you must do to achieve success? Do it now.

Don't use prayer as a crutch, as a way to avoid taking inspired action.

Do something. It will produce a result.

You'll be different at the finish. Act now.

Celebrate early success.

Week in Review (Take your time filling this out. At the end of a year, you can notice good change.)

Which of this week's quotes resonated with you most?

_____

_____

_____

_____

Why did this quote resonate?

_____

_____

_____

_____

_____

Write about early success you're experiencing. Add lots of detail.

_____

_____

_____

_____

_____

_____

_____

_____

_____

_____

Just You

Being yourself is success.

Love yourself and temptation to compare yourself to others vanishes.

This is your journey, no need to cover another's path.

If everyone else was an inch high, that wouldn't make you tall.

Comparisons interest us when we don't know ourselves.

How silly for infinite beings to engage in comparison.

What if the person you love wasn't there?

Week in Review (Take your time filling this out. At the end of a year, you can notice good change.)

Which of this week's quotes resonated with you most?

_____

_____

_____

_____

Why did this quote resonate?

_____

_____

_____

_____

_____

_____

Is there anyone you've been comparing yourself to? Why do you use energy to compare yourself to this person? How would you feel about yourself if you stopped comparing yourself to others?

_____

_____

_____

_____

_____

_____

_____

_____

_____

Patience and Persistence

Patience and persistence pay off.

Persist until your work is done.

How long? As long as it takes.

You must decide not to give up.

Two simple words hold immeasurable power - Keep Going.

Patience doesn't mean live in a paralyzed state, refusing to take one good step forward.

What if the next step takes you inside your miracle?

Week in Review (Take your time filling this out. At the end of a year, you can notice good change.)

Which of this week's quotes resonated with you most?

_____

_____

_____

_____

Why did this quote resonate?

_____

_____

_____

_____

_____

List 4 actions you'll take to become more patient and to stay motivated as you persist toward fulfilling your love-based goal.

_____

_____

_____

_____

_____

_____

_____

_____

_____

_____

Focus

How far away from you is your goal?

Focus until your goal is imprinted on your conscious
and subconscious mind.

When looking within you should see yourself fulfilling
your goal.

This way, that way focus calls.

Make your reward your aim.

Pay attention to noise and you won't focus.

Show me where you're focused, and I'll show you
where you're going.

Week in Review (Take your time filling this out. At the end of a year, you can notice good change.)

Which of this week's quotes resonated with you most?

_____

_____

_____

_____

Why did this quote resonate?

_____

_____

_____

_____

_____

Spend 15 minutes a day visualizing and feeling what it's like to live with your goal fulfilled. At the end of the week, write about how you feel as it regards achieving your dream.

_____

_____

_____

_____

_____

_____

_____

_____

_____

_____

More Than What You Do

You're more important than what you do.

Above the work, value You.

Dreams shouldn't take you away from your True Self.

Don't chase a dream to the point that you lose your Self.

Work is meant to be a way to get what you want, not a drowning tool.

Rest awhile. It's a smart move.

Your greatest reward is meeting your One True Self.

Week in Review (Take your time filling this out. At the end of a year, you can notice good change.)

Which of this week's quotes resonated with you most?

_____

_____

_____

_____

Why did this quote resonate?

_____

_____

_____

_____

Write about five traits you absolutely love about yourself.

_____

_____

_____

_____

_____

_____

_____

_____

_____

_____

"At its heart, learning is an awakening."

Chapter 6 – Keep Learning

To learn is to expand, to allow yourself to access an awareness of greater opportunities, pathways to success, and inner healing. You change as you learn.

Beyond learning, another choice that changes you is the choice to *sincerely pursue* your goal. A huge goal that you pursue causes you to see yourself differently. In time, you'll observe your real strength, inner vision, trust, and goodness. You'll see and feel this goodness, causing the part of you that doubts your goodness to yield.

In fact, there may be no more effective way in this world to awaken than to pursue *and achieve* a huge love-based goal. This is a goal that does no harm to you or any other living being. It could be a creative or artistic goal. It could be an educational, spiritual, scientific, ecological, or economic goal. The important fact is that, while pursued and once obtained, no one is injured.

As sweet as it sounds, pursuing a love-based goal is not enough to fulfill the goal. You must change your thinking and take the right actions at the right times to fulfill the goal. Somehow, you must make your way from where you are now to where you want to be.

That journey calls for learning. Afterall, if you already knew what to do to experience lasting success, you'd be there right now.

Continual Learning Within and Beyond Your Field

Learning is a part of success.

Learn not, want much.

Education expands your horizon.

Stop learning, then what?

This world is ever changing, so too is the need to learn.

The next thing you learn might hold what you've been looking for.

Learning is valuable if there's change.

Week in Review (Take your time filling this out. At the end of a year, you can notice good change.)

Which of this week's quotes resonated with you most?

_____

_____

_____

_____

Why did this quote resonate?

_____

_____

_____

_____

_____

What do you do to ensure you keep learning about your industry, market, passion field -- knowing that change is constant? Do you attend webinars, conferences, take online or offline classes, etc.?

_____

_____

_____

_____

_____

_____

_____

_____

_____

Certifications and Licenses

Certifications are a sign of what you've already learned.

The right licenses build customer confidence.

Identify certifications and licenses you need and you're partly there.

People want to know what you know.

A wise woman has no certifications or licenses.

Experience is more than certifications and licenses combined.

The smartest people only work in life's school, though that's not where the money is.

Week in Review (Take your time filling this out. At the end of a year, you can notice good change.)

Which of this week's quotes resonated with you most?

_____

_____

_____

_____

Why did this quote resonate?

_____

_____

_____

_____

Do your research. Which licenses and certifications are needed for you to achieve your goal?

_____

_____

_____

_____

_____

_____

_____

_____

_____

_____

Online and Offline Learning Options

Asking the right question is part of the answer.

Much learning is gained outside a classroom.

Better to learn virtually than not at all.

Online or offline, completing a course only works if you apply what you learn.

Combine what you learn with real life applications.

Open to greater learning opportunities and watch your mind expand.

The more you learn, the more you can teach.

Week in Review (Take your time filling this out. At the end of a year, you can notice good change.)

Which of this week's quotes resonated with you most?

_____

_____

_____

_____

Why did this quote resonate?

_____

_____

_____

_____

_____

Using the Internet, library, college catalogs, etc. search for and identify online and offline courses you could take to deepen your learning in your focus area.

_____

_____

_____

_____

_____

_____

_____

_____

_____

_____

Reading The Right Books

Books yield boundless success.

Inside a book is a harvest of opportunity.

Choose books carefully, their effects are deep.

Books are a wise woman's friends.

Unto each is a book that must be read.

The right books make the heart glad.

More knowledgeable you become with each book you read.

Week in Review (Take your time filling this out. At the end of a year, you can notice good change.)

Which of this week's quotes resonated with you most?

_____

_____

_____

_____

Why did this quote resonate?

_____

_____

_____

_____

_____

List 10 books that dig into the study and power of habits, beliefs, and your focus-area.

_____

_____

_____

_____

_____

_____

_____

_____

_____

_____

Always a Student

Always be a student.

***

The more you learn, the more you can teach.

***

See yourself as a student and you'll adjust to your industry's changes more effectively.

***

Where would you be if you had never learned anything?

***

Student! Student! Where are you?

***

A happy day is filled with learning.

***

Commit to learning and applying 10 new lessons toward your success each week.

Week in Review (Take your time filling this out. At the end of a year, you can notice good change.)

Which of this week's quotes resonated with you most?

_____

_____

_____

_____

Why did this quote resonate?

_____

_____

_____

_____

_____

Are you committed to continue learning? Why or why not? (Write about it.)

_____

_____

_____

_____

_____

_____

_____

_____

_____

_____

"Countless holy encounters have blessed your path."

Chapter 7 – Important Partnerships

All relationships have value. Each relationship is a holy encounter because of what created us and the fact that we are extensions of love and light. If you focus on an illusion of what you "appear" to be, you'll miss love; you'll miss the light – not only in yourself but in others.

Regardless of what you think or feel, the light is always there – always. Yet, as you pursue success, there are relationships you will need to enter and nurture. Some of these relationships may begin as unproductive partnerships. Others may start at a place where you see the reward in the relationship right away.

Between you and the next person who's key to moving you forward, closer to your goal fulfillment, might be no more than one to three people. Don't think so?

Do you know every relative of each colleague you work with, down to their second and third generation relatives? How about your neighbors? Do you know each of their relatives and, even more, each person those relatives know?

Even if you're an influential socialite, it's highly unlikely that you'd know hundreds of people mentioned in the above paragraph. Get to know people in your life more deeply and they may naturally introduce you to their broader circle of family and friends. Any one of these people could connect you to a key player in the market or industry you want to succeed in.

Any of these people could be the entrance to important partnerships. If you're wise, you'll value all relationships, not to avoid missing out on a key partnership, but because you value life. You love and care about all living beings.

The latter will empower your important partnerships with a genuine grace, the type of grace that engenders you to others and others to you. Love others as you love yourself so people know that you sincerely care, which by itself, can open remarkable doors of opportunity.

Mentors and Coaches

Mentors and coaches offer valuable, razor-sharp support.

Mentors and coaches offer valuable, razor-sharp support.

A mentor is proof that you can do what you're striving to do.

Insight is a gift given and received from a coach.

Build a team of quality mentors and coaches.

If you're serious about your success, partner with the right people.

A coach can help you see what you're missing.

Mentors and coaches believe in you when you've stopped believing in yourself.

Week in Review (Take your time filling this out. At the end of a year, you can notice good change.)

Which of this week's quotes resonated with you most?

_____

_____

_____

_____

Why did this quote resonate?

_____

_____

_____

_____

_____

If you've worked with a mentor or sponsor before, write about benefits you gained from the experience. If you haven't worked with a mentor, is there anyone you'd like to mentor you? Why? When will you reach out to this person, asking them to mentor you?

_____

_____

_____

_____

_____

_____

_____

_____

_____

Elders

Elders not only love you, but they also offer on-point life lessons.

Lessons elders teach stick.

Your biggest lessons may have happened at home.

Grandparents love and protect you with wisdom.

There are relatives who make learning fun.

You carry what you learned at home with you everywhere.

It's what your caregivers taught you that you won't forget.

Week in Review (Take your time filling this out. At the end of a year, you can notice good change.)

Which of this week's quotes resonated with you most?

_____

_____

_____

_____

Why did this quote resonate?

_____

_____

_____

_____

_____

_____

Think about your older relatives, including their career field, hobbies, etc. Which of these elders has insight, experience, contacts, etc. in your "dream" field?

_____

_____

_____

_____

_____

_____

_____

_____

_____

Your Inner Guide

Be led by your Inner Guide.

Trust your Inner Guide.

In the stillness you can hear your Inner Guide speak

You've trusted fear long enough. This time, believe in your one True Self.

Meditation is a call to the "real" you.

Writing down your dreams could encourage you to enter communion with your Inner Guide

Don't bet against your true Self. It's a sure way to lose.

Week in Review (Take your time filling this out. At the end of a year, you can notice good change.)

Which of this week's quotes resonated with you most?

_____

_____

_____

_____

Why did this quote resonate?

_____

_____

_____

_____

_____

Inner guidance always speaks with love. Write about the last loved-based action inner guidance prompted you with.

_____

_____

_____

_____

_____

_____

_____

_____

_____

_____

Crucial Relationships

Relationships are at the heart of all success.

Spend time with those you love. The payoff is huge.

Valuing work over relationships is an error.

Relationships will make or break your dreams.

The right relationships add joy to your life.

Wrong relationships extract strength from you.

Love has a splendor that's only realized in rewarding relationships.

Week in Review (Take your time filling this out. At the end of a year, you can notice good change.)

Which of this week's quotes resonated with you most?

_____

_____

_____

_____

Why did this quote resonate?

_____

_____

_____

_____

_____

Describe the 3 most important relationships in your life. Why do you appreciate these relationships?

_____

_____

_____

_____

_____

_____

_____

_____

_____

_____

Non-Physical Help

Everything you need to succeed is inside you.

Ask and the answer will surface.

A sincere call for help moves mountains.

All your help won't come in physical form.

Pay attention to guidance and insight that bubbles up within your mind.

You can't see your mind, yet it's working on your behalf right now.

Like success, you can't touch or hold the greatest help you'll receive.

Week in Review (Take your time filling this out. At the end of a year, you can notice good change.)

Which of this week's quotes resonated with you most?

_____

_____

_____

_____

Why did this quote resonate?

_____

_____

_____

_____

_____

Have you ever been helped in such a way that you can't describe all the help from a physical perspective? What was that experience like?

_____

_____

_____

_____

_____

_____

_____

_____

_____

"Appreciation is evidence that you've looked within and seen a spark of truth."

Chapter 8 – Appreciation Opens Doors

The human brain is given to habits and routine; it's a great way for the brain to connect neurons. Power up by getting into the habit of seeing the good within yourself, good the Creator placed within what you are in truth. This enables you to project the goodness you see within to others which causes appreciation to expand.

I learned this lesson a hard way. Years ago, morning after morning, I rose with a singular thought, "Oh, no, another day." It was as if I regretted waking to another day, expecting the day to fill up with struggle in no time flat.

That single repetitive choice blinded me to butterflies and frolicking squirrels for years. It also kept me from hearing birds singing. Today, that experience still shocks me. Don't let this happen to you, not if you want to advance in good ways.

Once I saw more fully what I was doing and how I was binding myself, I shifted into appreciation. Up my hands went. Open went my mouth. Words of appreciation and thankfulness poured out of me.

Soon afterward, I saw a butterfly for what seems to be the first time in 10 years. Talk about a welcome sight! And I saw squirrels running up and down trees in playfulness. The sound of birds singing was an outright treat.

That display showed me the strength of appreciation. Another thing I have seen appreciation do is to serve as powerful motivation.

Express appreciation to your Creator and yourself for each forward step, however small the step may appear to you. Doing so helps you to recognize the progress that you are making. That alone can motivate you to continue until you achieve your goal in fullness.

Where You Focus

Appreciation waters the good in life, causing it to grow.

⁂

Steer your attention toward appreciation.

⁂

Where are you going? Appreciation knows.

⁂

Love is inside you. Let it bloom with appreciation.

⁂

Your focus is a seed.

⁂

Looking within to your core is looking up.

⁂

Focus is a magnet, pulling you along.

Week in Review (Take your time filling this out. At the end of a year, you can notice good change.)

Which of this week's quotes resonated with you most?

_____

_____

_____

_____

Why did this quote resonate?

_____

_____

_____

_____

_____

_____

What has gained your focus this week? Does it align with your goal? If not, why do you keep focusing on this idea, experience, etc.?

_____

_____

_____

_____

_____

_____

_____

_____

_____

Count What Matters

Start counting your blessings. See if you can keep up.

Counting blessings encourages you to seek blessings.

Blessings are all around you. How many do you see?

What if the good you seek is part of you?

Let blessings flow like a gushing waterfall.

Your heart knows what matters.

Trouble be gone. I'm busy counting blessings.

Week in Review (Take your time filling this out. At the end of a year, you can notice good change.)

Which of this week's quotes resonated with you most?

_____

_____

_____

_____

Why did this quote resonate?

_____

_____

_____

_____

_____

List 10 blessings you've received this week.

_____

_____

_____

_____

_____

_____

_____

_____

_____

_____

Appreciation's Energetic Flow

Appreciation's root is love.

A sure link to happiness is appreciation.

It's not stagnant. Appreciation flows.

Where does your appreciation go?

Up! Up! Energy! Up into appreciation.

What do you love? Let yourself love it.

The dance of appreciation is sweet.

Week in Review (Take your time filling this out. At the end of a year, you can notice good change.)

Which of this week's quotes resonated with you most?

_____

_____

_____

_____

Why did this quote resonate?

_____

_____

_____

_____

_____

The last time you felt a surge of appreciation, in what ways did that appreciation change your energy / how you felt?

_____

_____

_____

_____

_____

_____

_____

_____

_____

_____

Don't Miss Blessings

Pay attention to what's happening in and around you or you could miss blessings.

Lack of appreciation erases blessings in a magical way.

Open your eyes. Your blessings are circling you.

One, two, three and four – count blessings as you spot them.

Celebrating blessings is empowering.

The good you're aware of is powerful.

If you don't feel you've experienced blessings, how can you be aware of them even if they are there?

Week in Review (Take your time filling this out. At the end of a year, you can notice good change.)

Which of this week's quotes resonated with you most?

_____

_____

_____

_____

Why did this quote resonate?

_____

_____

_____

_____

_____

Was there ever an instance when you missed a blessing for months, perhaps years? Write about it. What happened to make you finally realize that you'd been blessed?

_____

_____

_____

_____

_____

_____

_____

_____

_____

_____

Power of Appreciation

All by itself appreciation is formidable.

Let the door of appreciation swing open into love.

Combine appreciation with good life stimulating habits.

Glimpse the wonder of appreciation.

Appreciation never empties itself.

Let appreciation swell up like a ripe melon.

Let your home be a house of appreciation.

Week in Review (Take your time filling this out. At the end of a year, you can notice good change.)

Which of this week's quotes resonated with you most?

_____

_____

_____

_____

Why did this quote resonate?

_____

_____

_____

_____

_____

_____

Ever felt a continuous lack of appreciation, in the habit of fault finding or complaining? How did that make you feel? Ever felt appreciation? How did you feel then?

_____

_____

_____

_____

_____

_____

_____

_____

_____

_____

"Your emotions are a witness to what you expect to happen."

Chapter 9 – Expect Success

When you're pregnant with an idea – when you're truly pregnant with a successful endeavor – you naturally *expect* the experience to come to pass, to reveal itself in this world.

This expectation births an exhilarating emotion within you. Little tops feeling that you're going to get what you want, that a strong desire you have will be fulfilled. That wonder can extend itself across days, even weeks.

Then, experiences in this world start to jab at the exhilaration. Perhaps you have a disagreement with a colleague or a neighbor screams at you, demanding that you keep your pet dog out of her yard. Or maybe you learn that a friend recently gossiped about you, sharing details you'd hoped to keep private.

Specifics of the situation aren't a major factor. The shift from hopefulness to frustration is. Before long, you might start to think that the earlier thoughts and emotions of you succeeding were a lie.

If this thought-emotion shift is a pattern for you, it wouldn't be a shock if you started to believe that not only will you not win but that you can't win. Hence, you spiral into frustration.

Instead of slipping into the trap of believing that the success you want will, as it has in the past, evade you – expect success. Let the exhilarating feeling continue, allowing it to become part of your routine, folding into your natural internal landscape.

Expect success.

Actually expect success to happen to you. See yourself succeeding doing what you want to do. Feel yourself selling lots of your products and services every day. Listen to audiotapes or videos, using headphones, that instill success images and success language and beliefs into your mind, deep into your subconscious.

Live expecting success, tremendous success. Don't just daydream or nightdream about success. Take smart actions to yield success and use your thoughts and emotions to attract the good you want. Yes. Yes! Expect success!

Get Ready

Your success is coming. Are you ready?

Prepare yourself for the good you seek.

Prepare for success so it doesn't knock you off balance.

The success you seek is seeking you.

Part of what you're doing is preparing for success.

I'm headed for success and I know it.

Are you ready to shift upward and soar?

Week in Review (Take your time filling this out. At the end of a year, you can notice good change.)

Which of this week's quotes resonated with you most?

_____

_____

_____

_____

Why did this quote resonate?

_____

_____

_____

_____

_____

How are you preparing for how your life may change after your dream is fulfilled?

_____

_____

_____

_____

_____

_____

_____

_____

_____

_____

See It

Visualize the success you want.

Inner vision works like a reliable map.

Inside you is an unimaginable success. See it.

Inner vision is dependable.

See it. Feel it. Make success real.

Every time I see my success, I'm motivated to move forward.

Fancy yourself succeeding.

Week in Review (Take your time filling this out. At the end of a year, you can notice good change.)

Which of this week's quotes resonated with you most?

_____

_____

_____

_____

Why did this quote resonate?

_____

_____

_____

_____

List 3 resources you use to help yourself visualize success (e.g., vision board, deep wealth meditation tapes).

_____

_____

_____

_____

_____

_____

_____

_____

_____

_____

Success Amid Constant Change

Change. Change. Yet success remains.

Success morphs but doesn't evaporate.

Success is as constant as change.

Time can't dim success' beauty.

Let success expand with each breath of change.

Constant change. Yes. And constant success. Yes.

Climb the mountain of success. You can reach its peak.

Week in Review (Take your time filling this out. At the end of a year, you can notice good change.)

Which of this week's quotes resonated with you most?

_____

_____

_____

_____

Why did this quote resonate?

_____

_____

_____

_____

_____

Write about the change that entered your life after the last success you enjoyed. How do you expect your life to change when your current goal is fulfilled?

_____

_____

_____

_____

_____

_____

_____

_____

_____

_____

Aligning With Success

Align with the good that's approaching.

You must line up with the good you want.

Stand up until you're shoulder to shoulder with success.

Good is about to happen for you. Surprised?

Use your energy to align with success.

Let your inner guide escort you into a better world.

Goodness believes in your success. Do you believe in goodness?

Week in Review (Take your time filling this out. At the end of a year, you can notice good change.)

Which of this week's quotes resonated with you most?

_____

_____

_____

_____

Why did this quote resonate?

_____

_____

_____

_____

_____

Do you think you're in alignment with what you want? Why? If not, how can you get aligned?

_____

_____

_____

_____

_____

_____

_____

_____

_____

_____

It May Seem Normal

Your dream may be fulfilled in the most normal way.

Seemingly "normal" events become miracles.

Stop telling yourself your dream will only be fulfilled if the most shocking event occurs.

Every day is a miracle.

When did you stop seeing life as a miracle?

One day you will look back and see that loads of miracles fell into your life.

Normal has become the most miraculous thing.

Week in Review (Take your time filling this out. At the end of a year, you can notice good change.)

Which of this week's quotes resonated with you most?

_____

_____

_____

_____

Why did this quote resonate?

_____

_____

_____

_____

_____

Do you want your dream fulfilled or do you want to be shocked? Write about it.

_____

_____

_____

_____

_____

_____

_____

_____

_____

_____

"Celebrate to draw in more good."

Chapter 10 – Celebrate Wins

Celebrating love-based progress motivates you to keep going. This might involve you taking small steps. For instance, to celebrate filing a patent for a new product you developed, you might write a celebratory note about the filing in your journal, or you might simply allow yourself to sit still, enjoying the success.

This simple decision could keep you from becoming frustrated, angry, or depressed while you work to bring what you want fully to fruition. In fact, this recently happened to me. After checking my book sales, I started to wonder if my goal to create success as a full-time novelist was a mirage and would never be more than a mirage.

Before I headed outside for a walk then to the store, I saw I'd sold six books. Rather than to sigh, wishing that I'd sold more books, I allowed myself to feel happy with the fact that I had indeed sold books. I didn't rob myself of the opportunity to enjoy what I had done.

That single choice lifted my thoughts and emotions just-like-that. It happened in an instant; I shifted from doubting my ability to achieve the success that I wanted to believing and knowing that I would, regardless of how long it took, realize the success that I wanted.

Returning home from the walk and store, I created a new book ad on a different platform. Another thing I did was to put the finishing touches on the first draft of a new book I'd started writing weeks earlier.

That's the power of motivation. That's the power of celebrating wins.

Fortunately, you don't have to spend money or expend lots of energy to celebrate wins. You do need to acknowledge the progress that you have made. Another thing you need to do is to stop and *celebrate* what you've done.

You could meditate and appreciate the forward step. Looking at the success for 30 seconds and letting yourself feel how big and significant this seemingly small step is, especially considering how it connects to larger success, is another way to celebrate.

Other ways to celebrate wins include eating a food you enjoy, carving out an hour to engage in a hobby, hanging out with a friend or visiting a museum, natural park, or an event that you love. Get creative when thinking of ways to celebrate wins, including those seemingly small yet hugely significant wins.

Acknowledge What's Happened

Live like you know you're blessed.

———◆———

Share the good that's happening with yourself.

———◆———

Acknowledging good keeps the door to miracles open.

———◆———

Let your life give early success a nod.

———◆———

I see your success and I want you to know.

———◆———

This time I'm telling the truth. I'm a success.

———◆———

I won't repress what's happening. I'm winning and I know it.

Week in Review (Take your time filling this out. At the end of a year, you can notice good change.)

Which of this week's quotes resonated with you most?

_____

_____

_____

_____

Why did this quote resonate?

_____

_____

_____

_____

_____

Describe your dream fulfillment. Write about the success you've worked for and gained in detail.

_____

_____

_____

_____

_____

_____

_____

_____

_____

_____

Celebrate Each Forward Step

One step forward after another -- celebrate.

Dance! Dance! The good you worked for is upon you.

You're racing forward, into the sweet arms of success.

Celebrate the very first success.

The entire process is worth celebrating.

Stop. Don't take another step. Celebrate first.

Let celebration be your gear shift.

Week in Review (Take your time filling this out. At the end of a year, you can notice good change.)

Which of this week's quotes resonated with you most?

_____

_____

_____

_____

Why did this quote resonate?

_____

_____

_____

_____

_____

_____

List 4 ways you will celebrate each forward step.

_____

_____

_____

_____

_____

_____

_____

_____

_____

_____

_____

Power of Praise

It's a mystery how praise powers up miracles.

Wake up with praise on your lips.

Each rising sun is a reminder of the wonder of praise.

Nature sings with praise.

From each life praise should rise.

You're not alone when you praise.

Praise for the goodness that is the universe's and yours.

Week in Review (Take your time filling this out. At the end of a year, you can notice good change.)

Which of this week's quotes resonated with you most?

_____

_____

_____

_____

Why did this quote resonate?

_____

_____

_____

_____

_____

What do you do to praise the Creator for the goodness in your life?

_____

_____

_____

_____

_____

_____

_____

_____

_____

_____

Energy Rising

Energy is rising! Get ready for a miracle.

***

Who knows where you're going if not you?

***

Look up. You're there too.

***

Life is good. Do you agree?

***

Do what it takes to raise your energy.

***

Energy is never stagnant. It's moving. Shift it upward.

***

Each day make sure your energy is rising.

Week in Review (Take your time filling this out. At the end of a year, you can notice good change.)

Which of this week's quotes resonated with you most?

_____

_____

_____

_____

Why did this quote resonate?

_____

_____

_____

_____

_____

List 7 ways you work to keep your energy positive, gushing with love and light.

_____

_____

_____

_____

_____

_____

_____

_____

_____

_____

Time to Dance

Dance! You've entered a new success phase!

Don't hold back, denying progress - Dance.

Your inner guide is a witness to what you've achieved.

Winning is part of life.

Dance with an open heart.

Dance until you *deeply* feel what you've done.

Move to the music playing in your heart.

Week in Review (Take your time filling this out. At the end of a year, you can notice good change.)

Which of this week's quotes resonated with you most?

_____

_____

_____

_____

Why did this quote resonate?

_____

_____

_____

_____

_____

How big are you on celebrating? How can you learn to celebrate more thoroughly, acknowledging the good you do?

_____

_____

_____

_____

_____

_____

_____

_____

_____

_____

_____

"To trust is to allow your true Self to lead the way."

Chapter 11 – Trust The Process

There may be times when the road to success, especially as you near manifestation, feels tremendously uncomfortable. Keep going. Meditate, do chakra healing work, get out in nature in a safe environment and go for a walk, submerge yourself in a warm bubble bath, etc. Just don't quit.

This might surprise you, but you may rock between feeling like success is yours to feeling like you *only* believe you can succeed *because* you're suffering from delusion. Trusting the process, continuing to believe that you're going to achieve your goal, may feel like the hardest thing you will ever do.

Hence, the importance of doing visual work, meditating, celebrating wins including small wins, and taking smart actions. Daily choices that you take, including resting and not obsessing about your goal, are powerful. Although they may be "seemingly" small, each of these actions is strong enough to keep you going.

Another decision you must make is to trust the success process even when you can't see what's coming. Trust the process even when your achievements aren't as large as you'd like them to be.

Who knows? You could be hours away from another shift, moving closer to a bigger dream fulfillment.

Also remember that a part of you may always want more. Don't allow this part to cause you to feel like you haven't done anything good as it regards your goal.

No. Don't do that. Instead, look back to where you started. Look at -- actually see -- and recognize your successes. Avoid cheating yourself out of acknowledging what you have done.

The purpose of this isn't to feel special or better than anyone else. Looking back at what you have achieved builds trust in yourself and trust in the Creator. It helps you to trust the process more fully. And it's within the trust that the fulfillment of your greater good rest.

Look Back – Look Forward

Revisit the process. See what's happened?

Thе one time to look back is when you've entered a
new success phase.

Achievement should not be ignored.

Look back and connect the dots.

Yesterday's struggles have become today's success.

It's no small measure what you've done.

Add up all the forward thrusts and see what's occurred.

Week in Review (Take your time filling this out. At the end of a year, you can notice good change.)

Which of this week's quotes resonated with you most?

_____

_____

_____

_____

Why did this quote resonate?

_____

_____

_____

_____

_____

Have you ever looked back over your life and felt *certain* that you could do *more* good? Write about one such experience.

_____

_____

_____

_____

_____

_____

_____

_____

_____

_____

_____

When You Can't See What's Coming

Your wish may surprise you when it shows up.

Success may startle you, showing up when and how you least expect it.

You are not seeing all that's happening behind the scenes.

Just because you can't see it, doesn't mean good isn't coming.

Stay calm with success.

Brighter days are ahead.

Good is coming as you beckon.

Week in Review (Take your time filling this out. At the end of a year, you can notice good change.)

Which of this week's quotes resonated with you most?

_____

_____

_____

_____

Why did this quote resonate?

_____

_____

_____

_____

_____

How can you boost your faith when you can't see your dream being fulfilled behind the scenes?

_____

_____

_____

_____

_____

_____

_____

_____

_____

_____

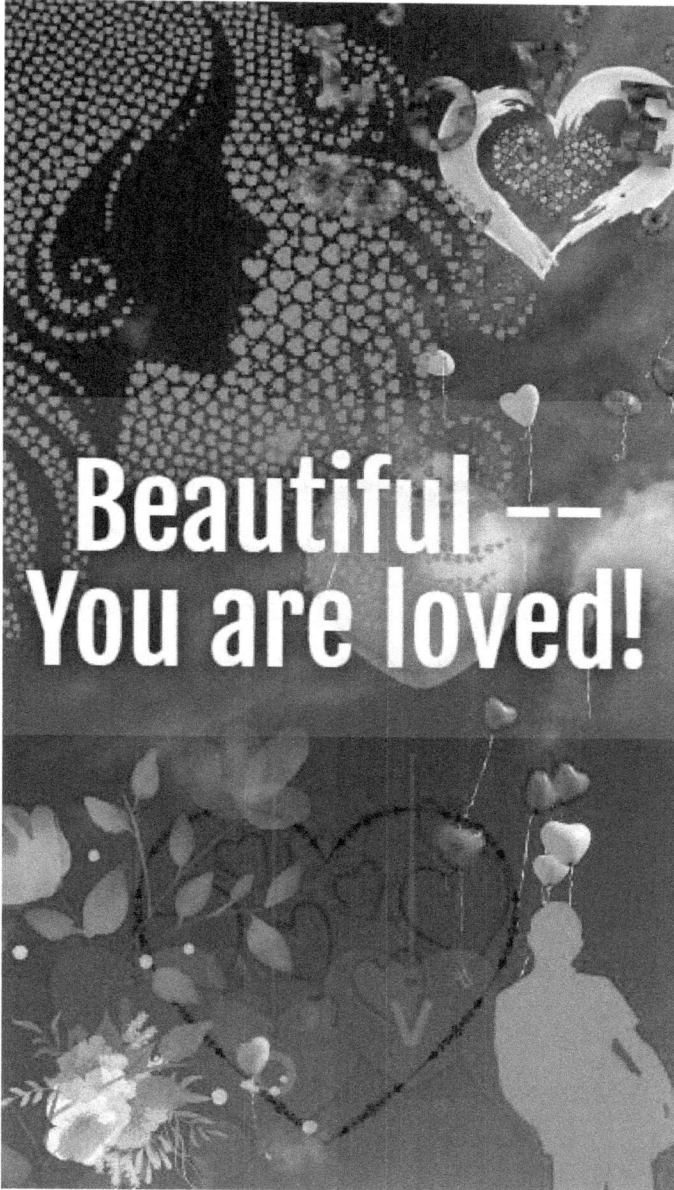

Beautiful --
You are loved!

Read More Books- by Denise Turney

Love Pour Over Me

Portia (Denise's 1st book)

Long Walk Up

Pathways To Tremendous Success

Rosetta The Talent Show Queen

Rosetta's New Action Adventure

Design A Marvelous, Blessed Life

Spiral

Love Has Many Faces

Your Amazing Life

Awaken Blessings of Inner Love

Book Marketing That Drives Up Book Sales

Champion! Your Will to Win is Key!

Love As A Way Of Life

Escaping Toward Freedom

Whooten Forest Mystery: Ties That Bind

Heal Gorgeous: Wisdom Within You Knows The Way

Thriving While Raising Happy Kids as a Single Mom

It Starts With Love: A Mother's Love Never Dies

Visit Denise Turney online – www.chistell.com

www.ingramcontent.com/pod-product-compliance
Lightning Source LLC
LaVergne TN
LVHW051054080426
835508LV00019B/1867